# JACK AND THE BEANSTALK

# JACK AND THE BEANSTALK

Retold in Verse
for boys & girls to read themselves
by Beatrice Schenk de Regniers

Illustrated by Anne Wilsdorf

Aladdin Books, Macmillan Publishing Company, New York

For Andrew Bellow,
That charming fellow!

First Aladdin Books edition 1990

Aladdin Books
Macmillan Publishing Company
866 Third Avenue, New York, NY 10022
Collier Macmillan Canada, Inc.

Printed in Hong Kong

A hardcover edition of Jack and the Beanstalk is available
from Atheneum Publishers, Macmillan Publishing Company.

10   9   8   7   6   5   4   3   2   1

Library of Congress Cataloging-in-Publication Data

De Regniers, Beatrice Schenk.
   Jack and the beanstalk/retold in verse for boys and girls to
read themselves by Beatrice Schenk de Regniers: illustrated
by Anne Wilsdorf.
   p.   cm.
   Reprint. Originally published: New York: Atheneum, 1985.
   Summary: Retells in verse the old tale of the boy who
climbed a beanstalk, killed a giant, and won a fortune.
   ISBN 0–689–71421–1
   [1. Fairy tales. 2. Folklore — England. 3. Giants — Folklore.
4. Stories in rhyme.]  I. Wilsdorf, Anne, ill.  II. Title.
PZ8.3.D443Jac  1990
[E] 398.21 — dc20   89–18663   CIP   AC

Here's a story about
A boy named Jack,
Bold as brass,
Sharp as a tack.

It's also about a Giant—
    Not very bright,
    But mean and BIG.
    In just one bite
    He can swallow a pig.

But what this wicked Giant
    Likes most
    Are boys—and girls—
    Broiled, on toast.

Jack's father was dead.
Jack lived with his mother.
He had no sister.
He had no brother—

But he had a cow
Named Milky White.
She gave milk every morning.
She gave milk every night.

By selling the milk
The cow was giving,
They were barely able
To make a living.

One morning, Jack's mother
Woke him and said,
"Milky White won't give milk,
And we have no more bread.

We have nothing to eat.
We will surely die."
Jack's mother
Began to cry.

Jack said,
     "Cheer up, Mother.
     Dry your tears
     And save your breath.
     I'll never let us
     Starve to death.
     I'll get a job
     In a grocery store."

     "No one will hire you.
     We've tried that before,"
     Jack's mother said,
     And she cried some more.

Jack said,
        "Now Mother, stop!
I'll sell Milky White,
Then we'll set up shop
With the money we get.
Don't worry, Mother,
We'll manage yet.
I'll take Milky White
To the market today!
Come now, Mother,
What do you say
                to that?"

"Oh, Jack!
What do you think
You can sell her for?"

"Ten pounds...twenty...
Maybe more,"
Says Jack.
"No one can cheat me.
I'll soon be back."

And off he goes with Milky White.

Jack hasn't gone far
When he meets an odd
Little man on the road.
Jack gives him a nod.

"Jack, I wish you good morning,"
The little man says.
Jack makes a deep bow.
"I wish you the same."
But Jack wonders *how*
The man knows his name.

"Jack," says the little man,
"Tell me, now,
Where are you taking that
Skinny cow?"

"I'm off to the market
In the city
To sell this very,
Very pretty
Cow,"
        says Jack.

"Jack, if someone does buy her,
He's sure to cheat you.
You're lucky, Jack,
I happened to meet you.
Let's see if you have
Your wits about you."

Then the man snaps his fingers:
"All right, Jack.
Look alive!
Do you know how many
Beans make five?"

"Two in each hand
and one in your mouth,"
Said Jack—
Bold as brass
And sharp as a tack.

"Right!" said the little man
"Well, I never!
Jack, I'll give you five beans
Because you're so clever.
I'm ready to trade them
Here and now.
You take my beans.
I'll take your cow."

"Go along,"said Jack.
"Do you think I'm daft?"
Jack shook his head.
The little man laughed.

"Jack, you're smart,
I've no doubt.
But it's plain you don't
Know much about
                    beans.

These are *magic* beans.
Give them a try.
Drop them on the ground,
They'll grow to the sky
                    overnight."

"Up to the sky?"

"Guaranteed!
If not, I'll give back Milky White."

"Agreed!" said Jack.
The man made a bow
And disappeared.
So did the cow.

"Hi ho!" said Jack.
"I may as well
Go home and tell
The good news to my mother."

"Why, Jack,
You're back!"
                    his mother said.

"You've sold the cow!
Jack, tell me now,
Tell me, what did you sell her for?"

"Mother," said Jack,
"You'll never guess!"

"Ten pounds?
Twenty?
More?
Or less?

Now Jack, don't tease."

"Well then, Mother,
Look at these
Wonderful,
Mystical,
Magical
Beans.
Give them a try.
Plant them tonight,
They'll grow to the—"

"Jack! You fool!
You pumpkin head!
Take that! and that!"
His mother said.
She smacked his face
(But not too hard),

Then threw the beans
Into the yard.

"Get out of my sight,"
His mother said.
"Go upstairs
And straight to bed
                without any supper!"

So Jack did as his mother said—
Went to his room, got into bed.
Sorry and sad he was, to be sure,
Because he had disappointed his poor
                    old Mother.

He thought he heard
His mother weeping.
Poor Jack had a
Hard time sleeping.
                He was hungry, too.

Now it's morning.
Jack awakes.
He takes
A look around the room. He
Wonders why it looks so gloomy.

Jack jumps up,
Puts on his clothes,
Then goes
To the window.
What does he see?

Something leafy and green...
Is it a tree?
No. It's—

"It's the biggest beanstalk
I've ever seen!"

                says Jack.

"The magic beans
My mother threw
Into the yard
Took root and grew
and grew
and grew

          up to the sky."

So Jack
        Opens the window,
        Jumps onto the stalk
        And begins to walk—
        Or rather, to climb.
        He climbs,
        and he climbs,
        and he climbs,
        and he climbs,
        and he climbs,
        and he climbs.
        He doesn't stop
        Till he reaches
        The top
                of the beanstalk.

And there
        Jack sees a road
        Straight as a dart.
        "Well, if I'm going,
        I'd better start,"
                        thinks Jack.

So he walked along,

and he walked along,

and he walked along.

At last
    He came to a house—
    A great big tall one.
    (A Giant's house?)

And on the steps
    He sees a woman—
    A great big tall one.
    (A Giant's spouse?)

"Good Morning, Mum."
Jack is polite.
He's hungry, too.
"Could you give me a bite
                    to eat?"

The great big tall woman says,
    "So it's breakfast you want?
    Well, it's breakfast you'll be
    If you stay around.
    My man is a giant.
    I can tell you that he
    Doesn't play around.

    His favorite breakfast—
    The one he likes most—
    Is boys (or girls)
    Broiled, on toast."

"Oh, Mum, I'm so hungry
I don't mind
If I'm broiled or baked.
Be so kind
As to give me something to eat—oh, please?"
Well, the Giant's wife was not so bad.
She led the lad in, gave him bread and cheese,
And milk in a mug.
Jack felt very snug for a moment,
                              and then...

Thump! Thump! Thump!
The house began to tremble.
The plates began to jump.
Jack's milk was spilled,
And Jack was filled
                    with fear.

The Giant's wife said,
 "It's my old man!
 Where can I hide you?
 Heaven help you
 If the Giant spied you."

She pointed to
The oven door.
"Quickly! Jump
In there before
    he sees you."

In comes the Giant.
Oh, he is big!
In one hand
He holds a pig.
In the other hand
He has three more.
"Wife!" he says,
"Broil all four
              for my breakfast."

Then the Giant sniffs:
"Well, well!
What's this
I smell?

Fee-fi-fo-fum,
I smell the blood of an Englishman.
Be he alive, or be he dead,
I'll grind his bones to make my bread!"

The Giant's wife said,
    "Nonsense! You're dreaming.
    Or perhaps
    What you're smelling
    Are the scraps
    Of the little boy
    You ate last night."

    "Mmm. Yes," said the Giant.
    "I think you're right."

The Giant's wife said,
    "Now darling,
    Go wash your hands
    And comb your hair.
    And don't forget
    Behind each ear.
    I'll have breakfast
    Ready, dear,
            by the time you're back."

And now, here's Jack
Peeking out
The oven door.
"Get back! Get back!
Wait till you hear
The Giant snore,"
           says the Giant's wife.

"After he eats,
He takes a snooze.
That's the time
For you to choose
         to leave."

While Jack waits,
The Giant eats,
Then goes to take
Two bags of gold
Out of a chest.
The greedy Giant
Does his best
To stay awake
and count his money.

Now counting money's
Very boring.
So very soon the
Giant is snoring.

The oven door is opening!
Now Jack is creeping
Quietly across the room—
Escaping while the Giant is sleeping.

As Jack is slipping past the table,
He grabs a bag of gold,
Then runs as fast as he is able
straight to the beanstalk.

Jack drops the bag.
The bag falls *plop!*
Into his yard.
Jack doesn't stop—
No time to waste.
So, breathing hard,
He climbs in haste,
Down, down, and down.
At last Jack's home.

Jack gave the gold
To his mother and said,
"You see? I'm not
Such a pumpkin head."

"And Mother," said Jack,
"Didn't I tell you
Those were magic beans?"
His mother said, "Well you
                                    were right."

At last the gold was gone.
So then
Jack climbed up the beanstalk
Again.

He didn't stop
Till he reached the top
And then—
He walked along that road again,
And he came to that great big tall house again,
And there was that great big tall woman again.

Jack asked her for something to eat again.
"Well!" says the woman. "It's you again!
Do you know—something very queer—
The very day that you were here,
My man missed a bag of gold."

"Hmm. That *is* very queer," says Jack.
Then he says (bold as brass and sharp as a tack),
"I think I could tell you a thing or two
About that gold that would interest you."

The Giant's wife was about to burst,
She was so curious. But, "Feed me first,"
                                    says Jack.

So she lets Jack come in the house,
Gives him something to eat and something to drink.
What will Jack tell the Giant's spouse?
Jack eats *very* slowly. He can't think
                        - what to say!

Suddenly, Thump! Thump! Thump!
The house began to tremble.
The plates began to jump.

The Giant was coming in the door.
Everything happened just as before:

Jack hid in the oven, just as before.
The Giant said, "Fee-fi-fo-fum," just as before,
And ate four broiled pigs for breakfast, just as before.

And then
The Giant said, "Wife, bring me my hen!"
The Giant's wife did as she was bid.
"Lay," said the Giant.
The hen did as told
And laid an egg
Of solid gold.

Then—just as before—
The Giant falls asleep
And begins to snore.

Quick as a wink,
Quiet as a mouse,
Jack grabs the hen,
Runs out of the house.

"SQUAWK!" goes the hen.
Now the Giant's awake!
"Wife!" he shouts,
"Why did you take
My golden hen?"

"What, dear?" she says.
"What did you say?"

Jack, by now,
Is far away.
In fact, he's home—
Home at last.
(He climbed down that beanstalk
Fast!)

His mother said,
"Thank goodness you're back!"

"Mother, I've something
To show you," says Jack.

Jack says, "Lay!"
The hen does as told
And lays an egg
Of solid gold.

Jack says, "Lay!" again,
And the hen lays another
Golden egg. "Jack," says his mother,
"I know this hen well.
It belonged to your father.

"You were only
Six weeks old. You
Don't remember, and
I never told you...

How
A wicked Giant
With his wicked wife
Came and took
Your father's life.
He'd have eaten you
And killed me, too,
But we hid in our copper pot.
So the Giant took your father's hen,
And he took your father's golden harp
And all the gold that we had got."

Well,
It wasn't very long before
Jack decided to try his luck once more,
            up at the top of the beanstalk.

"This may be the very last time
That I'll be making this dangerous climb,"
                    says Jack.

So he gets on the beanstalk,
and he climbs
and he climbs.
And he doesn't stop
Till he reaches the top.

Jack knows that now
He'd better hide
From the Giant's spouse
And find a way to slip inside
The Giant's house
            when no one is looking.

Now who is there behind that tree?
It's Jack! He's waiting until he
                is sure the coast is clear.

And now it is!

Jack creeps inside.
 He sees the oven,
 Shakes his head.
 Decides to climb
 Instead
 Inside the copper pot—
 And just in time!

 Thump! Thump! Thump!
 Here comes the Giant again.
 His wife comes, too.
 "Fee-fi-fo-fum" again.
 "Wife, don't you
  smell him?"

The Giant's wife says,
 "If it's that young lad again—
 The one who took your golden hen—
 I know where he is sure to be.
 Just open that big oven door."
 Now Jack hears the Giant roar,
  "LET'S GET HIM!"

Thank goodness, though, Jack isn't there.
They cannot find Jack anywhere.
The Giant and his wife forgot
To look inside the copper pot,
                    Thank goodness!

Jack sees the Giant sit down to eat,
Then call for his after-breakfast treat:
"Wife, bring me my harp of gold."
The Giant's wife does as she is told.
"Harp, sing!" says the Giant.

And the harp sings a lullaby
So delightfully
That soon the Giant is
Snoring frightfully.
"That's my father's harp," says Jack,
"And it rightfully
                    belongs to me."

So,
        Quick as a wink,
        Quiet as a mouse,
        Jack grabs the harp,
        Runs out of the house.

The harp calls loudly,
"MASTER! MASTER!"
The Giant jumps up.
Oh! Disaster!
Jack runs fast.
The Giant runs faster!!

But Jack has a start,
And he knows the road leads,
Straight as a dart,
                    to the beanstalk.

The harp calls again,
"MASTER! MASTER!"
(Jack holds the harp tighter,
Climbs down faster.)

The Giant is getting mad and madder;
Swings down onto the beanstalk ladder.

Jack feels the beanstalk shake.
He hears the Giant roar.
But now he sees his mother
Standing at the door.
                    He's almost home!

"Mother! Mother! Bring the axe!" he calls.
His mother runs out with the axe,
Then trips and falls.
Jack jumps down,
Grabs the axe,
And then, *whick-whack*,
Jack hacks and hacks
and cuts the beanstalk through.
The beanstalk falls.
The Giant falls, too.

Miles away some farmers found
The giant dead upon the ground.
An ugly sight.
Most people think it served him right.

What happened to Jack?
Well, Jack and his mother,
As you may have guessed,
Had all they needed
For all of the rest
                    of their lives.

Jack married a princess, so people say.
And, I am told,
To celebrate their wedding day
Jack gave the princess a big bouquet
Of bean blossoms—made of solid gold.

There's really nothing more to tell,
Except that all went very well,
And they all lived happily ever after.